A Concept of Right Now

Poems by J. Scott Walker

A Concept of Right Now

Poems by J. Scott Walker

A CONCEPT OF RIGHT NOW
Copyright©2019 J. Scott Walker
All Rights Reserved
Published by Unsolicited Press
Printed in the United States of America.
First Edition 2019.

All rights reserved. Printed in the United States of America. No part of this book may be used or reproduced in any manner whatsoever without written permission except in the case of brief quotations embodied in critical articles or reviews.

Attention schools and businesses: for discounted copies on large orders, please contact the publisher directly.

For information contact:
Unsolicited Press
Portland, Oregon
www.unsolicitedpress.com
orders@unsolicitedpress.com
619-354-8005

Cover Design: Kathryn Gerhardt
Editor: Rachel Warren
Editor: S.R. Stewart

ISBN: 978-1-950730-01-8

Contents

The Winter Witch	9
If Heaven Were a City of All White Buildings	10
Sweet Sonia	12
In Anticipation of the Summer Solstice	13
I Dream of Making Salsa in the Himalayas	15
Asia	18
I Pray to the Rats	20
The Chalk Sea	24
A Concept of Right Now	26
Siddhartha Looks at the River	28
Upon Hearing the News of the Death of a Student: Natasha Porter, 1994-2009	31
Saltwater	33
Sleep Visits Me	34
Zelda	37
A Student Asks Me How You Know When You Are In Love	38
Upon Hearing the News of the Death of My Aunt: Linda Bolton King, 1958-2013	46
G-R-O-C	48
You Are Not Expected to Complete the Work	50

A Concept of Right Now

The Winter Witch

She is the poison luck
of long dark January.

I am the apple core
de-fleshed by sharp teeth.

She is the noon hour
when the light is low.

She is the white muse.
I am the crow of sunrise.

She is a birch branch spindle
hanging as in a death.

I am the hemlock root
shriveled in a twisted wind.

She is the long primeval valley sleeping
under a galaxy of bones and bleak truths.

I am the lies the stars tell the eyes.
She is the comfort of needles.

If Heaven Were a City of All White Buildings

In Memory of Rebecca
Hatcher's Pass, AK

I.

Under the cover of the minute hand
of a great clock is an avalanche.

And trapped underneath the snow?
Time: Is it so unbelievable?

The boreal owl paints the silent moon
with his song; obscured by the change

from summer milk to winter milk
those clouds are the eyelids of the night.

There have been darker days
but none so soundly sleeping.

If the raven is afoot
he has not shown himself

but the tender shoots are missing
and the coins on the eyes of the dead spent.

II.

If heaven were a city of all white buildings
and the trouble of remembering

left to each soul upon arrival
there would be no contrast

between the endless snow
and the houses of loved ones

whose memories slowly vanish.
In the twisted-up fog

that covers Becky's face
beside the window

all that falls to ground
are moments lost

by those on Earth
not terribly worried about tomorrow.

Sweet Sonia

*Found poem from **Father of the Four Passages** by Lois-Ann Yamanaka, pp. 122-123. (New York: Picador, 2001).*

In an alley in Pusan
a man eats by a sidewalk

where the boiling swamp cabbage
and mung bean sprouts tangle. He watches

a frenzied dance, what looks
like a fish head ants tread

a winding path near. Soup steams;
embers crackle. A dirty little boy

tends to a small tabby cat
distracted by the marching militia.

Roaches scatter. The little boy
is picking white maggots out

of the cat's eye, popping worms
with one fingernail.

He sings a delirious song.

In Anticipation of the Summer Solstice

Anchorage, AK

What belongs in the city but the grime
on the hands of the anchored man

and the oil rig that spews what he gathers
settling deeper into the mud April left?

A lone flugelhorn told him to drop
his own free will and sink with the lot

of the surrounding buildings. It was
a miner's tune after the gold rush.

Nothing gleams quite like
the afflicted banks of a river

of words and in some spaces
there is no sunset, only evening

that lasts, and its colors that don't
and shouldn't are prayers: *Requiem!*

It is a new year now for the dead
who've stopped counting, whose

cowboy hearts have been thrown
sidelong from the broncos of lust.

The diamond roads cut by our forbearers
shine like sweet lies against the razor truth

of the Chugach mountains. Green of this city
is just the color of the wood that survived

the hatchet, and a bare tree inhabits the evil spaces
we cannot see in the damp and din

of the untouchable mind saying:
What doesn't kill you makes you.

I Dream of Making Salsa in the Himalayas

after Agha Shahid Ali

The five of us forge a pact:

To have the words we make
taste just as they sound

in our kitchen high up
in the Karakoram Range

and to gather the ingredients
each in bowls of carved balsam:

Habaneros aged in October sunlight
parched and soured by a cool dry wind
that sings of the monsoon's absence

juice-red tomatoes the dog himself
has brought in. He cares for them
gently plucked and placed on the stoop
as payment for his supper.

> *The important thing*
> *is to let each ingredient*
> *speak something no*
> *other can. Stir.*

And who will slice the onions?

Not one in five prepares
to bear the burden.

And who shall sing a raga thanking
Allah for what the Lord has given?

      the Rasta for his sativa
      the Buddha for
      the Great God Pan

O, Shahid, you've arrived just in time

to take this knife
from my trembling hand,

to calm the roiling
water down, to add:

Confetti peppers sizzling in oil
in a copper sauce pan, the orange
pieces bleed to pink, red to white

black beans and corn dance
between rising bubbles. We leave
them until the salted water
softens their skins.

      It's fine to let the pot boil
      over, to listen to the music
      the steam makes rising
      but not for long. Cover.

And who will be the first to taste?

Five pilgrims hoping
to place salvation

on tongues rinsed

in merlot and amnesia.

Many hands reach
but for a single bite

and none but Shahid
remembers to smile

when speaking the agreed upon
invocation:

> *I never thanked my mother*
> *for giving me this recipe*
> *and it will soon be too late*
> *to teach the ones I love.*

Asia

Do you see the minarets
of Constantinople? Do you see

her blue water? Her Black Sea?
She has an open heart.

We traveled incognito
through Turkey via France

danced in a fountain in l'aeroport
until a constable shushed us away.

Asia, you laughed at his ten-cent
mustache; I tried to lift his pillbox hat.

In a mosque in Aleppo
we walked across the blue-green tile

trampled the cuneiform script written
into each stolid brick.

They worshipped you for a moment,
Asia, like a storm rises.

Your curve, the shadow of a minaret
falling to a sea where light pools

waiting for the sky to swell. Your skin
the lee shore of an island in monsoon.

That night, we vanished before we could be
found in a crowd in New Delhi. You said:

Why does the moon search for us if only
just to deny the hour of our lingering?

We floated on streetlamp silk
to a little café where a madwoman

served us Russian vodka
until we fell asleep.

In the morning we woke to the smoke
of street market vendors: Sprigs

of lamb on wooden skewers.
For breakfast we shared a jar of candied

pears stolen from the governor's secret garden.
The yellow sugar melted in your hot breath.

Asia, you opened a window
and walked through.

I Pray to the Rats

I.

...and this is the world's greatest sadness:

that the meek shall inherit the meek
and the bold shall die defending
their blindness

and neither shall inherit the earth
for now, for those who are not human

to rediscover our humanity
it is necessary to abandon
what we know of it.

And so, god of many gods

I pray to the rats
in hopes that they
will remember:

Peril is in the pupil of the pulpit.

In the not-so-distant humming
of some final autumn

the pupa of the great hornet of the age
lies sleeping, waiting for its wings.

It is an angry, stinging sleep.

II.

Strange, how greed and righteousness
go so easily together in the minds of children.

Theirs is a logic most obscene:
Truth's dirty fingerprints arriving
on yesterday's papers, language
laced with the anthrax of apathy
borne into the body through some
divine scandal.

Civil war breaks out
among the utterly reptilian holdings
of an American soul: fear, rage
suspicion, and a silent hatred
founded on ignorance.

And to think we could have pulled
ourselves back

from the self-same precipice
quite some centuries ago
and the dogmatic certainty
of objective truth

before the forfeit of freedom for safety

when language still had the potential
to illuminate, to transcend, to begin
the great human awakening.

III.

O, the minions will labor
to build a deficit of knowledge
O, the ministers will call out the moments

as each painted prayer peels
away in the all-too-severe
offices of a real world
of competing virtues:

The rabid appeal
of absolute sophistication
of competition not cooperation

of salvation by self-invention
and the internal conspiracy—

the unholy engineer inside us
passes into shadow but leaves behind
his hulking machines—

preservation by self-mutilation

which have their spades and axes
and their piercing us is what we tell
ourselves makes us good.

How carefully we writhe inside our skin.
How playfully we stab each other daft

in the darkest places of our minds
to teach ourselves to mistrust
the universe.

But rats don't mistrust the universe.

They nibble at its edges
shaping it in their way.

And they are there, out-chewing us
despite our best efforts to dull
the teeth of all animals.

The Chalk Sea

Night pours out the hours
like soft rain dissolves
into clouds of fog and snow
and yellow leaves. Only
the cold hands the city
sits upon to warm can tend
white mountains into drifts
of lost sheep. Look, up against
the window, how chalk
people in chalk dwellings
mill about in false light;
their shadows of red
and blue—dust from a fireplace
or television—reflecting back
in signals usually only seen
at the tops of very tall buildings.
Of trees the wind makes
an excited loom, spinning the yarn
of winter into frozen cocoons
that rest in motionless branches.
The sky is an ecstatic green web
where eight-legged things
seem all at once hatched
and moving—chalk creatures
returning to chalk lagoons. Look
out beyond the reach of day
how even the dirt moving in the tide
is of the same white stuff that chokes
the early morning air and settles
into everything. Thin beams of noon

make a chalk eye out of the chalk
moon and life no longer stirs
where the chalk valley
spills forth into the chalk sea.

A Concept of Right Now

I.

Time is what repeats.

The atom's tick seizes 100 million
years without fail. What time is it?

What is time? It is what time is.
Synchronizing our lives in a station, it is

the realization that Einstein, immutable,
discovered one's own private time

moving-unmoving.

II.

On cusps of moments we don't experience
in dimensions that exist and are obliterated

time is the unfolding of a paw before it hits snow,
the residue of light in any direction.

Do we agree on what's happening
out the window?

III.

The present isn't nonexistent; a frozen river
is never really locked in place.

Too small to notice, gravity tugs on time.

I didn't age; she aged fifty years. She went
back to Chicago, but not by going back.

IV.

The contradiction of God is reversible
in the laws of physics. We all know

what happens when a glass of wine
cannot achieve what the arrow of time

prevents: a neatly ordered book
undone by entropy.

V.

The puzzle is not complete; completeness
is the puzzle. We should expect to find

ourselves in the middle of nothing.
The past is out of reach

out of reach without end.
There is no change.

Siddhartha Looks at the River

I.

He can see in its
machinery
the end of everything.
To Siddhartha, memory
and time
are in its essence.

And the end, merely
a continuation
of some primal
perpetual
beginning.

At this, he laughs
for it occurs
to him that the river
dies away
in the memory of man
at the same speed
at which
it arrives and always
in the same
direction.

II.

He contemplates
the lotus
blossom being carried

downstream
and the fighting salmon
gaining
and losing in the curl
of an eddy.

They pass once.
The lotus steady,
constant, still.
The salmon, its body
wrenched
in high arches like
solar flares, falls back
to the water
washes downstream.
They pass
again.

III.

Siddhartha thinks
of the alignment
of the earth, moon
and sun, the eclipse
of the lotus
and the smatter-shine
of water droplets
in forest light.
They pass
again.

IV.

He does not think
of Sisyphus—
Sisyphus naught of him.
They do not
know of one another.

This is why he has come
to the river:

To see what
can be seen
and not see what
cannot.

He is resigned
to go.

Upon Hearing the News of the Death of a Student: Natasha Porter, 1994-2009

Her mom killed her
    but not with hands
        only words, only

wishes. No, it was what
    Natasha did, lashing out
        last and worst

at the only thing
    she ever truly owned:
        her bare white neck.

It wasn't quick or painless
    and pointlessly we all
        said we never

had a clue what
    had made her do it
        besides what makes

anyone play so violently
    with a noose. Mere
        mercy the child

sought to end the vile
    buffets and blows
        of a world so scornful

as to say which
    person a person
        was allowed to love.

And though we all wept
        bitterly inside
                it was the resolution

of the tragedy we all
        carried and our cathartic
                bliss lasted longer

than the memory
        of the heartbreak of the girl.

Saltwater

That drowsy mid-summer's night
        on a white sand beach

the offshore moonlight kicked
        in our faces made us feel

intricate and impoverished
        regarding one another

in the frog-ridden mud. In darkness
        and in wind they stirred

then settled. I made them a house
        you made them a castle.

I gave them watermelon rind fences.
        You let the saltwater drip

from your toes down into their eyes.
        They were already crying.

Sleep Visits Me

I.

In a dream you press your body into mine
a sweet sensual risk I can know only this way

in the first low rays of daylight, lying
on a dock beside an ocean in midsummer.

It is not strange that you should touch me
at this hour. It seems only like the hand

of destiny and sad as if we know the moment
of true awakening will shatter the house

of whispers we have built together in our mind.
And know, as well, how the hint of birdsong

and the smell of empty wine bottles
will wash away in the tide when it comes.

II.

Silhouettes darken the under-lid of my fluttering eye.
Reality seeps in random

and uninvited. In all the patterns established
by the plague of sanity that teaches us

in our ignorance to ignore what we cannot deny
we can only hope to forget this encounter

or push the memory of it so deep that it would
never occur to the next generation to dig it up

and place it in a collection of pieces
in a museum, ancient artifacts

of a thing once called love.

III.

In another dream you stand beside
a road in a tree-lined square, a place

both modern and eternal, watching me move
the way a person does running from

the possibility of painful death that threatens
to swallow up the world and you.

And though it isn't death I am running from
but the specter of a life lived

in a monochrome parade just passing by
the fear is almost equal to the emptiness I feel

when I realize you're not here, never were
never would be.

IV.

In the throes of passionless night
I think of you and sleep visits me.

In the permanent state of being
that crashes in on a solitary mind

at critical mass I think of you
and sleep visits me.

In the vacant places of my heart
scraped clean by the spade of regret

I find you and sleep visits me.
In the afterthought of every thought

and in the forethought of the mind we share
within a celestial fold of time-travel unimagined

of space travel pure and undefined
I think of you. I think of you

and hope to touch you once again
in a dream.

Zelda

Zelda was a family dog, blue as black
ears the size of pigeon wings
antennae for the life she dreamed:

to find the white clouds rustling
and chase them away, far forever.
Yet she lingered, content and timid

until Chow Jerry, the neighbor dog
taught her to trowel under fences.
We've not slept a night since she

last got loose, free as flame
eyes flickering in glossy dog thought.
Three days hunger brought her home

but never again would she stay.
Winters, more nomad than houseguest
Zelda came with leaves brown as black

roaming to wherever spring winds call.
Today's blue sky reminds she's gone
her absence felt where nothing floats

overhead but heaven, bothersome as ever.

A Student Asks Me How You Know When You Are In Love

I.

I tell him a love story
one that ends in heartbreak

one that ends with me doubled over
on my side in a teenage bed weeping

because I didn't know how to kiss her
and nothing happened.

I tell him, I tell all of them,
that I had given my heart to a girl

that I had chosen her and hadn't
even realized that I had done it

until I realized that she hadn't
and never would. I tell them

how I still feel that ache
after so many years and how

you sometimes don't know
what you want until you know

and by then it's too late.
That's when it occurs to him, to all of them

that this shit is no joke
that what we are doing is real

and that what happens to a person
in life stays forever.

Because in that moment
they can see forever

through me into my past
and understand

that it is their own past
which they have not yet lived

and their own love
which they have not yet lost.

And they weep, inside of course
for me, for us, for us all. And I know

by how silent they are
that they have never really considered

how silent love is.
How silent. How brutal.

Love is not a feeling.

II.

There will be a woman
and she will draw you in

with her sea-foam eyes
rolling like waves swelling

and spraying and in them
you will drown so sweetly

that no prayer for death
can sweep you back

to shore. She will smile
and you will shudder.

She will tell you she thinks
about you when she is alone.

She will sweep her hand across
your shoulder blade or collarbone

and accidentally press her body
into the palm of your hand.

She will make you want her more
than she wants you in the end

and that is when you will step back
and realize that you are lost in a hall

of stolen glances with a different
truth reflecting back in every mirror.

But you will go gladly, blindly
through the maze of her

to see if there is a center
where she's taken your mind

to stake your heart
and stuff it back in the box

of demons she released
it from in the first place.

And there you will be, in the caustic
embrace of damned fortune smiling

a whitewashed prison with many
windows, no bars and no roof.

Love is not freedom.

III.

You will find yourself walking
in a wood of pale yellow autumn

alone, or so you think, with the parchments
you have scribbled in a half-mad attempt

to see the rain for what it is:
A grey mood you have called in

with your ablutions
with your incantations

sung for a mighty god
who listens but doesn't hear.

The one who hears is the one
for you and she will wait

for the words on the undersides
of the fallen leaves—

the confessions you have left
for anyone or no one to find—

to appear within her gaze
where she measures you

from a distance before
approaching like one who

would handle a wild
injured dog. She heals you

and promises to keep you
safe for years until you find

yourself at the edge of something
sharp and steep. Will she

push or pull you back? Will
she see you twist and tumble

down a narrow chasm
of pride and good intention?

Or will she be the one rope
that helps you climb out again

fallen and forlorn? These questions
are a poem. The poem is inside you

hiding its little voice from the world.
Will you let it out?

Love is not knowing.

IV.

Take care to be the man
you want to be for her

the one who lays your head
inside her lap and props

up the pieces of your broken
skull with tattooed hands.

On them is written in a script
of ancient wisdom, a story

known only in the esoteric
movements of a dancer

spinning on the pinnacle of epochs
balanced on the points of a million stars

converging in one mad moment.
Don't resist the moment, be in it

and be it for the love of love
for all things desert

need all things river
just as all things soil

need all things air. What
would a life be without pain

without emptiness, without night
without dirt, blood, and mothers?

What would this wandering be
without death to call us home?

Would you die for her, young man?
Would you be the one rabbit

running headlong into the tooth
and claw of watchful destiny?

Would you be the singularity
of me us we you and time?

Don't be afraid to love, I say.
Be afraid not to. Be afraid

of a feeling of freedom and knowing,
but do not be afraid to love

as you should not be afraid to die

for love is the death of death and you
will know it in her every syllable

and in the very breath she draws
to speak your name and in the life

that leaves her lips as her every
moment passes into you.

Love is a word.

Upon Hearing the News of the Death of My Aunt, Linda Bolton King, 1958-2013

It wasn't that early or late
    when the coyote howled you out
        of the middle of sleep.

You said your last goodbye
    with the imprint of his voice
        still sweet on your cold lips.

Your last thought was of a face.
    Everyone's last thought is of a face.
        The face you thought of was

your mother's. Your last memory:
    how you played in the ocean
        the day she died.

A fog of dispassion hung on you both
    like a wreath of jay feathers, fleshy
        merlot apples, and pine straw.

You will not go to see any god.
    In the end, she will come to you
        as a mother mountain lion

solemnly protecting the last
    remaining cub on Earth:
        Was it not also the lesson

learned by Gilgamesh when he returned
    home without the rose
        of everlasting life?

It was always something
        you understood: We are the tragedy;
            you, the hero.

G-R-O-C

Albemarle, NC 1986

August green swells in a rare
wet season.

Kudzu fingers reach across
dust roads

in plain sight of a rash, angry sun
whose balmy light

squirms, trapped on the horizon
in folds

of thick-quilted
atmosphere.

My grandfather walks me down
past Tar River

across town to his public space:
Six tomato plants

and a lovely brown-skinned woman
he secretly wants

to marry. She introduces me to her
son, a shaggy-head

kid who says he can Jordan.
He's all street

but a ghost of anger doesn't live
in him like it does in me.

He never eats lunch on a Friday
in July just to save

money for sneaks and gambles
with dice whenever

his older brother lends him a dime.
We walk

to the G-R-O-C, but he says he won't
go in there—

the twisted flag of another America
hangs in a window—

and that I shouldn't go either—

a terror I had never known seized
me through him—

on account of he was
the N-word

and I was a N-word
lover's boy.

You Are Not Expected to Complete the Work

It may no longer be enough to say
that all that burns was meant to drift

by in front of our eyes in a wind of waste
and want. It may no longer be enough

to cage the stars and tell ourselves
the eyes of wolves don't speak

with tongues half-consumed by mere anarchy.
Remember that there is no poem that has not

been written and no stone that has not
been upturned in the pursuit of the knowledge

that lies buried in the tombs of a thousand-thousand
mothers' sons. Their blood

is the ink still wet on this page. It is in us
to prevail just as it is in us to fail.

Take care to name all things as you see fit.
Take time to tell those you love the name

you have chosen just for them. Be ever awakened
in your mind and in your heart

and know: Everything you fear will come
to pass. Everything you touch will break

mend and splinter. Everything you hope
to be will fade. Everything you dream

will materialize in a universe within and without
of the reality you perceive.

You are expected to fight and you are
expected to die, but you are not expected

to complete the work.

Acknowledgements

Poems in this collection have appeared in the following publications:

"The Winter Witch" Town Creek Poetry, Fall 2014.

"If Heaven Were a City of All White Buildings." Cirque, Winter 2013.

"I Dream of Making Salsa in the Himalayas." Cold Mountain Review, Fall 2013.

"Saltwater." Cold Mountain Review, Fall 2013.

"Poem in Anticipation of the Summer Solstice." Big River Poetry, July 2013.
   --Poem of the Month for July 2013.

"Asia." Big River Poetry, July 2013.

"Sweet Sonia." The Orange Room Review, August 2013.

About the Author

J. Scott Walker teaches English and Creative Writing in Greensboro, NC. When he's not doing that, he writes songs, plays, and poetry. A graduate of Appalachian State University and the University of Alaska, his poems have appeared in *Town Creek Poetry*, *Big River Poetry*, *Cold Mountain Review*, and *Cirque*. The emphasis on place in his work is the natural product of having lived in ten US states including both Carolinas, Pennsylvania, Nevada, and Alaska. He has also travelled extensively outside of the US both in a physical sense and also in his imagination.

About the Press

Unsolicited Press is a small press in Portland, Oregon. The small press is fueled by voracious editors, all of whom are volunteers. The press began in 2012 and continues to produce stellar poetry, fiction, and creative nonfiction.

Learn more at www.unsolicitedpress.com.

www.ingramcontent.com/pod-product-compliance
Lightning Source LLC
Chambersburg PA
CBHW030134100526
44591CB00009B/651